T0113568

ADVOCATE POETICALLY:

SCHOOL REFORM

J.S. CHRISTIAN

authorHOUSE®

AuthorHouse™
1663 Liberty Drive
Bloomington, IN 47403
www.authorhouse.com
Phone: 833-262-8899

Published by AuthorHouse 03/19/2022

ISBN: 978-1-6655-5543-2 (sc)
ISBN: 978-1-6655-5542-5 (e)

Print information available on the last page.

This book is printed on acid-free paper.

ADVOCATE POETICALLY: SCHOOL REFORM

JUST IN CASE

JUST IN CASE
They can't play basketball.
Or run fast
Around the track at all.
Or sing and dance
Let's take a chance.
And educate our kids.

JUST IN CASE
A chase to catch
Falls short
Of the scouter' s match for any sport.
Let's academically work out.
And educate our kids.

**When math and science
clearly seem.
The best recruiter and best team**

Let's shift implicit bias back
Include all students
And all facts
Please EDUCATE ALL KIDS.

EXACTO

When you take the time
to do it
Take enough to
Do it right

If you get it right
the first time
You won't
Have to do it twice

So no matter what the
IT is
Clear concise and careful
Plans

Provide the path
calculate math
to do it right
Again

SAY CHEESE!

Back and forths do not occur

in isolation.

U.S. sneezes, England cheeks in

"God bless you!"

Power on cell can easily tell

We are on camera
We are global

Leading social linkage to...

Little Joey in Kentucky

sharing snapchats

of the new pet

bearded dragon

he named Ace

With a kid in Cameroon hoping
to know one day soon
Why a lizard lives in such
a fancy place.
(and indoors!)

FIVE FEET

I think in
iambic pentameter
The reason not clearly
Known why

Thoughts flow
In five beats

Rhythm is replete

The teacher said this
Was a lie

PET PEEVES

Proudly looking

Over the mess

he planned and

ran to evil do

Styrofoam blood

from teddy bear

Wicked agenda

For those shoes

Denied (yea Lied) he knew of it
Then hung his head in shame

Claimed the cat and gerbil did it
Causing discord with the blame

Seven!
Committed all
Of them
Promise
Never do it again!

Thank God
Pets aren't
accountable
Like us humans
when they sin.

(Once)

I can clearly recall

disrespecting my parents only once.

Transgressions after then

were all blurry.

APB

Put out an

All Points Bulletin

For those suspects who

Come packing their ambitions

And full entitlements to ...

a home, good education, domestic
tranquility,
rights to happiness, due process, life and
liberty,

and any church of worship.
With or without seating.
Put out an APB for
All People Breathing

WE POE

Me and Edgar Allan
Poe

Pour hearts out
in the words

Placed in our minds
So all could find

Inspiration heard

Me, Edger Allen,
Poe
Riches come from
prose

A wealth of verse
Exhumed, rehearsed
Poetry
Juxtaposed

Rewards?
They come in
Heaven
Countless artists
Know

Frugal fame
Fraternity
Me,
Edger Allen,
po’

P. E.

Help us, Lord, to stop doing this
Predatory Exclusion.
It hurts our kids

Those things we do delude deceive
And sort afford split who receives

Rights intended fair and just
Are meant to include all of us

Even disabled
Oh Heaven forbid!

Promontory PEACE instead
which too impacts the kids

NORM

Why are we still living in
Norman Rockwell art?

Education

Eduhateshun

The picture has gotten old

THE MESSAGE

Sometimes when you rhyme
The message is so sublime

The meaning through the meters thwart relaying

There is movement.
It's off beat.

Coerced words forced;
can unseat...

Peace notes' message
the messenger is saying

So, although a pulse for rote,
Listeners need able note

Understand what it is
Rhyme writes to say

IS

**We must educate
End HATE
StartingToday**

(SIC) PORPOISE

Perhaps we spend
Two much tyme fuzzing
about how bess
disseminate

School fonding muny dollars
used to awl kids educate

Besize the languige
Looks much cuter
When we type it I. R. L.

I.D.K. what the porpoise is
No, reely. I cain't tell

T.T.Y.L. but I.D.K. from where
With such stunted knowledge

L.O.L. if you think it will be while
Inside any college

SCHOOL NEWSFLASH

There is enough education for everyone.

An excess as matter of fact

So much knowledge is held in the library books

We had to up layer in stacks

Look anywhere and everywhere there is something new to know

Discernment does the channeling

What, when and how the knowledge goes

The good news is, yes, all
LEARNING OVERFLOWS!

BRIGHT KIDS

The sunlight of knowledge
dispersed K through college
Some receive light
Some wither away

Unless loved enough
to grow strong
smart and tough
Education can remain at bay

Kids need to have facts and formulas imparted
Epistemologically

Enough to thwart falling;
felling like trees

Enough to thwart failing.
Try.
Please.

DEAR LANGSTON

Dear Langston,

You asked me, the Master of questions, what happens when dreams are deferred?

Let's say they never wake, for deference sake. Slumber seems the dream venue preferred.

They mushroom in darkness. Grow through the night. Not festering.
Awaiting...
the kiss of sunlight.

So, why did you pose question prophetically?
Just say it.
Is there something
inside you can see?

Love,
Me

HIDE N' SEEK

When you close your eyes we still see you.
Prolonged
Doing so
You can see
Us in
Nightmares
And Dreams.
The best thing it seems
Is to wake up and stay woke.
Knowing…
We're not going away.
Here we are
Here we'll stay
This is no time to play
Hide and Seek.

(Here)

Here is better than the sidewalk

Here is better than the street

Better than drugs

Pull a chair up

Let the children have a seat

(in class)

LESSONS LEARNED

You teach me
like you like me
I learn like
You teach me
to like me too

You teach me
like you hate me
and I learn like
You teach me
to hate me.

And You,...

Who holds the keys to
knowledge, academics,
cards to college

Who to and who not to listen to

You taught me
the opposite
of what not
loving learning
could be

Signed,
a former student,
PhD

HUSH

People with something to say

Often don't in fear

Someone may be listening

To what everyone should
hear.

TORTOISE V.
SHELLED HARE

In the ongoing case of Shell-less Tortoise v. Shelled Hare

Starting line is wide and level
Starting guns startle some there

BANG!

Course map is same for everyone.
Route carved out as it should

Determining determination. Over
str8 paths through the woods.

Then course markers noticed punctures
on the Tortoise back

where cover was removed at times along the arduous track

The shell had dents and paw prints.
Graffiti "you're too slow!"

Tortoises don't talk.
There was no way for us to know.

The hare used as umbrella then, Tortoise shell, as shield...

To protect and project himself.

Your Honor, help us if you will.

"In due time.
Race is in Progress.
The jury is out still."

A DICTION

"The choice of words and phrases in
your speech and in your writing"

Just imagine if all chose words only
focused on enlightening.

Because there can be
A diction
Minus angst
And absent hate

Genesis of goodness.
Loving words
Perpetuate

Saying and acting kindly
Until a Habit
Is Inviting

Imagine World:
A DICTION
Uncontrollably
Uniting

MATHEMATIC SOLUTION

Hate times hate
Is hate squared
Times one more hate
It's cubed

Multiplied
It replicates
Regurgitates
Renewed

Hate added
Just reflects itself
Division
Does the same

Subtracting
Is the only way
That hate
Can be contained.

MISSING SCHOLAR

Can you help me find Samantha? She
sat in the seat right there.
A small Brown girl with dark brown curls
Disappeared into thin air.

Can we try to reach Samantha?
Can you tell me where she went?

She came to school like other kids

To learn, to grow, to mark present.

Caboose. Never line leader. Went
out last and held the doors.
While classmates laughed and socialized.
She did the classroom chores.
She never missed the parties
She was not invited to.
Learned protocol by all means all means
everyone but you.
"Samantha banana brown girl from Havanaaaa"
Actually hailed from Carlsbad.

Always ignored and quite often bored.
The bullying made her quite sad.

Ashley P. to the left drew mean faces.
Ashley K. did the same on the right
Both invited, included and full attituded.
Found fun in provoking to fight.

Samantha always raised her hand first.

To answer the questions. Compete.

Against Ashley, just one, who enjoyed making fun
As they sat in the star gifted seats.

Samantha's zeal was marginalized quickly
Then disordered as ADHD.

While Ashley's was lauded and often
applauded preclusion to a PhD.

Samantha one day just stopped coming
rest assured what it was
about
Scholar oxymoron coercion
Ensures all smart brown students get out.

Can you help me find Samantha ?

(Gift)

Be the gift.

Can you spare one more

invitation to the party?

THE REVEAL

Since the world is now aware From
the many ways we share

Some apparently formed impressions of their own

They whispered all amongst amidst

She told her then he told his

How we have done our data all along.

Now they know the undertow
Has arisen
Overflowed

The united of our states
May be a rouse

Because we still won't
Free our Education loose

It is a privilege not everyone can choose.

POETIC PULSE

Poetry
requires readers
to breathe.

Without
Readers
Poetry
Has no Pulse.

APPLAUSE

There are a group of people who decided

Knowledge should be imparted not derided

They cheer students who have the gifts

The ones with challenges uplift

Then cheer them too

They care enough to share the skills
they learned for each

With hopes somehow the
child
is within reach

For learning due

Knowing 100 percent matter,
to help the child then nation better

TEACH

NO RIGHT TO EDUCATION

Brown v. new brown generation
New musicians misspelling same songs,
Educashun
Educasion
EDUCATION
is a
Privilige
Privalage
Priveledge

Privileged **PRIVILEGE**

Not Right; some try
With disabled deny
How could this ever go wrung?

SENTENCE

Mom has to make it through her sentence and
His sentence

Without crying so that she
Can try explain

In time that's left
Her son is deaf
and signing signing
trying trying (not defying)

NOT defying!
when
the officer exclaimed...

CONTRACT(UAL)

Take notes to craft a contract with
~~pathetic~~ parenthetical voids
Appease to garnish signature.
Get funds. Coerce. Destroy
Call meetings then ~~feign fake~~ make
emergencies on a parent time
Then proceed to craft a contract
filled with a lot of ~~LIES~~ lines
"We will teach your children (not)
to enrich their minds
We will be fair (ly) impartial
always nice and kind
(of)
Equal encourage (meant)
will always try to try
Treat all children just the same, ~~except~~ accept disabled".

Why?
Not trusting what was ~~meant~~ made to sound sincere.
"Ignore parens, typos and strikeouts.
Just sign here".

EXPONENTIALS

Seeds grow into saplings
Saplings grow to trees

Kind thoughts grow kind actions
Kindness grows world peace

Smiles grow into laughter
Laughter grows to joys

Education grows strong minds
Hope for girls and boys

Strong minds know to plant seeds
Seeds know they must grow

Kindness; exponentially
beyond status quo

AXIOMS

Hate requires action to become a verb.

Silence cannot be misquoted.

Mirrors reflect.

Hearts can detect...

When childhood dreams are

Imploded.

RETORT

Julie hated losing.
She punched
the new brown
girl named Kay.

Kay was smarter, cute, and witty though
was unsure just what to say.

When Julie called her the n- word,
it echoed around the world

Kay was silent, taught non-violence, so didn't hit the girl

(on the playground)

Kay stood still in contemplation

then replied with a retort

"Middle school has kiddie rules.
I will see you one day in my court."

MATH TEST

M.ake A.ccountable t.o H.onor

T.eaching

E.very

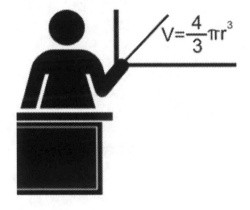

Student

Truth

HANDI

Fund tether them tightly.
Reach out and hold.

Teach them the ways.
Give means to grow old.

Handicapped children
grow up to be

Handicapped grown ups
who still are in need.

LITMUS TEST

After many years of college
Having acquired degrees of knowlege

Voluntarily your own major chose

Congratulations for achievement
A noble cause for those
Believing
Children in need can benefit
from what you know.

Behaviors are all grounded.
The experts have all found
diagnosis and the
circumstances vary.

It is deep, thus there is need for those with capabilities to
step up
step in and
In Steps carry

Genuineness helps the children
No matter what the kids' hue is
Don't cash checks for work you know you did not do

The litmus test is in the tether to the child who does get better
From what diagnoses experts say are true

Manifestations are the calling, it helps the kids so please stop stalling. Give CARE due

The litmus tests are testing, child growth and funding tethers

Education
Children,
and the nation getting better.

WHO COUNTS?

Count them in and
things could happen
Count them out and
you are in trouble
Count them wrong
you have to ask them
Exactly which box
do you bubble?
Count as 1/2 or 1/2 then double?

CORED

English is our spoken tongue

Science explains what was done

Math adds it all up in summation

Social Science gives narrations

KNOW SANTA

In his defense
He waited all year
Then waited in

Very long lines

No one there dare rush him
He had a long list
And relaying would take
A long time

To see Santa
'Twas Christmas
This is what his gift was -
To speak for the deaf
See for blind

He researched the choices
For ones without voices
For the ones without legs
Who can't climb

Braille books made with mixtures
of smooth and rough textures
With shapes cut to teach
Squares and rounds

And sensory toys
ASD girls and boys
Can be easily startled
by sounds

Throw in giant bucket
colorful sidewalk chalk
That's for baby brother
He can't talk or walk

Kid, others are restless!

(Wish they wouldn't balk.

This isn't for me,
I'll just take world peace
And a little more patience
Behind)

Santa said,

"I can't bring that.
Kid, you just need Jesus.
He does well with crowds
and long lines"

(1 Flag)

Even gifted kids can barely

understand discrimination.

After pledging their allegiance

to a flag for the whole nation.

CARLSBAD DECREE
LAMENT

Carlsbad circa 1819.
Brotherhoods all in collusion.
News and students are muffled or caste out.

School bells should have warnings. Truth for all would be
alarming
what Carlsbad's Decree was all about.

What if we pay our taxes?
What if we mow our lawn?

What if we
What if we
What if we
What if we

Tell you we sound alarms?

What if we bring you bundt cakes?
What if we wave hello?

What if we
What if we
What if we
What if we

Tell you that we all know...

Some of your long-held secrets...
Most of your long told lies.

Choosing to vengeance bully
Means educate deny

Why won't you
Why won't you
Why won't you

Why can't you

Look us all in the eyes?

How can we be your neighbor?
How can you not cause harm?

Why must we
Stay away

Why must you
Why must they

Threaten us with their arms?

Why when some kids test "gifted"
Scrutiny must be done?

Smart; too much
Smart though just
Hue's askew.
Legal thrust.

There has to be something wrong.

**no IDEA why disabled. pay for those who
mislabel. and your own. this is wrong. going
on. way too long. Violate IDEA; hurt.**

Why do you down diversing?
Why do you hate-crime fight?

Children need
Harmony
Others see
Country bleed

How do you sleep at night?

You're gonna call this fiction
Seems you can't handle facts

What do you
What do you
What do you
What do you

What do you think of that?

COME WITH LANTERNS

Hold up a light to the darkness.
In darkness the shady ones live
Prey on the weak
Label as freaks
To take and to take and not give.
Let's shed some light on these bad guys.
Call them cowardly. Victims. Make cry.

When they're caught, isolate as the spreaders of hate.
Place labels and don't even try.
To include them with all of the non-bullies.
Then name call. Cheer angst and pick fights.
Grab your lanterns, go get them!
Stop them, don't forget them!
Reflect bullying isn't right.
(By bullying?)

PARENTAL GUIDANCE

Kids used to play outside.

A lot of other kids were there.
Some fun was there was
Little parental supervision.

Kids are now back inside

Friends have video games,
virtual bonds with strangers,
F- bombs,
Violence
Little Parental Supervision

No worries.

At least they're safe.

FLIGHT 380 TO
BIRMINGHAM

she was, when it happened,
neither for nor against.
just napping...

because she could.

they were, when it happened,
neither for nor against.
all laughing...

as children should.

she was, when it happened,
missing kids bible study because flight 380 delay
then **bump!** plane landed
then **boom!** church exploded

she was grateful her plane arrived late.

NOTHING NEW
FOR SIOUX

We spoke in two different languages.

We beat of two different hearts.

You felt entitled to stay, kill and take

We wanted you to depart.

You called it Manifest Destiny

We called it heartless and cold.

The trails of tears
terrors and fears

Nothing settled

STOLE.

DEAR KINDER,

Little Scholar Skylar,

Can you go run me an errand?
You're much younger
will be stronger
and can reach

Much farther in the future
As you go, I can ensure
you'll grow dendrites
From the lessons that I teach.
Grab a crayon, take some notes.
Never take for granted
rote,
or the Abacus

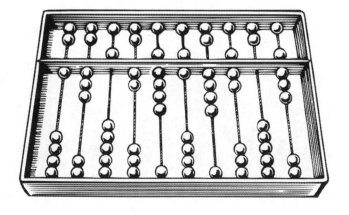

or any boring speech
I'm just laying
the foundation
for you to grow
and run...
THE NATION
standing on
learning
lessons
that I teach

WINNING MINDS

When intellect contradicts melanin content;

B.S. Oxymoron. Oh my!

If a few are let in then
supremacy ends

And equality may go awry.

Man your stations, coasts, schools, and your status

Scholars rise above block walls and gates

Armed with the Almighty's Handbook of Highering.

Winning!
Pitting love against hate.

AFFIRMATIVE (DISTR)ACTION

Imagine running 10 extra miles to the start
of a marathon.

You painstakingly
complete all 36.2

However,
your finish
Is forever
marginalized
Due to the color
of your shoes.

(yeah, it's like that)

DEAF EDUCATION

She says she wants to
make a living.
You want her to
make a sign.

We're thinking education.
You're just mocking, marking time.

We hear depth and intellect.
Researching class at Yale.
You have hate on speed dial
to take from schools to fail.

We know of aspirations.
Big future dreams and goals.
You're counting down 'til
she's 18 years old.

RINDS

The tough outer coating
of sweetness inside.
Projecting and flavoring
all over time.
Decide how the future will taste

Protecting, impacting
fragile young minds
Imagine the impact
the future will find.
In fruit juiced with kindness not hate.

MEMES SCHOOL

Glancing at the seating charts in newly reformed schools.
Still in alpha order. Very confusing rules.

No pictures. Confidential.

No cameras. Minors there.

Can't reform the old way
with germs everywhere!

Let's just meme them,
make it all seem fair.

STEALING BASES

Heaven help the Robbing Hooders
Who by day chant songs of praise

Of themselves for all the
hard work
and e-funds selfless raise

For their own kids' school tuition
Disabled children's caste aside

Faking CARE now camera rolling.
Then misappropriate. Tell lies.

Making jokes of kid's expressions
Mocking movements to frustrate

Casting shame on least amongst
US.
Should repent before too late

DICTION

Practice using real words.
Taste them before you say them.

If lyrics are sour or profane,
don't bother to play them.

Ponder what words' purpose is.
If there is none, be quiet.

Inciting ones just kill the fun
and that's how we start riots.

SUM LAUDE

Daddy says can still dig
Ditches
With a PhD.
Try earning without learnin'.
See whut yer options be.

And, watch your mouth!
Don't go south.
Run from doom and gloom

Do good and well.
(Remember)
Can't change a thing
Outside da room.

LOVE IN MONEY

Let's have U.S.A. civil reunion
Down in Money, Mississippi

Round up all
same surname mix
families
Unveil
Genealogic history

This is the place we lost Emmett
Scarred by bryant history wounds

Time for healing museum for teen boys we (k)need
to come see and reconcile soon

Let's name

"Till Tomorrow"

for Emmett

Since lost all of his yesterdays

Old men can design it,
young men can come build it,
young boys can come help out (and play)

Love brings together.
Time helps heal Forever
ForEveryForever
Today

MATURITY

Unashamed of her behavior
Unaware when coming on
Though some staff will
sadly laugh
just like the students poking fun

The more mature are empathetic
understanding neurons fail.
Disabled need more
understanding
not laughter, ableism, jail.

The more mature were empathetic
sympathetic unafraid
To stand apart and stand up for then
stand against games bullies played

NOT GUILTY

I wasn't even born then
My grandparents owned no one
I invited most of my classmates
to my parties; out for fun.

I mean, so not everyone could
Come inside my house to play

I could meet them at the
local park
And whenever they...

Would invite me over their house
I had something else to do

It was not because of race.
Well, mostly true.

HYPOTHESIS

Sparking ideas fuels ambitions
Crushing ideals is foreboding

Mirrors reflect
Truth
with respect

To childhood dreams
as exploding

KIKI'S GATE

This one's for
Kiki Flack
Who always had
too much to say.

When the teacher tried
to hold her back, said

"No ma'am...I don't play!"

Refrain from
Relegation
To remedial
Because

Implicit bias
Leads you there.
Though, in the past,
It was...

OK to subvert
Intellect
To the effect-
Subdue

Ambition borne
Of retrospect
From my ancestors
Who...

Were Mocked
and
Marginalized by
People just like you."

Not anymore!
No longer.
The world's
Being rearranged.

Let's RIGHTly
Provide
Education.
Constitution;
Change

INTERLOCKING PEACES

Puzzle pieces fit together because their edges are shaped
to either interlock or lie smoothly alongside one another.

Fence.

People populations
piece peace together
with interlocking edges and ideas
smoothly alongside one another.

Intense.

Mocking the interlocking by
Staying connected is not puzzling.

It beautifully.
makes picture perfect sense.

WEALTH

Hope you are never too rich to accept kindness

Or too poor to not have some to spare

The giver and receiver both benefit from actions

These actions grow from having just been there

So, for the sake of kindness

Perpetuate giving blindly

So all can see

true wealth

you have to share

PERPETUATION

Some do some same things for so long

They forgot fact those things are wrong

So long it has somehow become

their mindset mantra

Motivation

Song

THANK YOU

Thank you Lord

For this Day

And every thing

It brings my way

And thank you for

A voice to pray

You'll guide my thoughts

And what I say

As I listen and obey.

CHOSEN OUTFITS

The group of us decided long
before training began,
That right was right, not
Black or White.
Good guys should always win.
Most of us still know the difference.
For all of us, there are
judgment calls.
It hurts when bad guys get away
And that the good ones
sometimes fall.
We promise. Promise. Promise.
No one signed up to heed a call
other than protect and serve,
protect and serve you
One and all.

JUST LIKE YOU

School Kids
Groceries
Taxes
Headaches
Heartaches
Backaches
Neighbors
Barking dogs

Spouses teachers
Church preachers
Grandkids
Chasing
Hurrying
Worrying
Writing
Daily Logs
Have great senses of humor; most
Yes, cops are just like you!

CONFESSION

I'm not because I've never been
The guy who keyed your car
The one who flipped you off
that time
Outside O'Malley's bar

The guy who poked your tires,
hacked your Calendar.
Yeehoo!

Who knew right timing
for a vandal.
you would be gone a day or two

It's just hearsay, never happened
if not seen with your own eyes.

There is not and has never been. A crime.

What cameras?
Oh, crap, you recognize?!

ENGAGEMENT

"Just try and stop me!"

Oh, I don't have to try
Though I'd much rather you comply.
We both go home to see our mates and kids

"And if I just go?!"

That could actually work.
Less mess, a lot less paperwork
More likely you listened to
what was said.

Let's take a breath because we can
Take a moment. Understand.
This exchange has a story
that began...

Something happened, escalated
Doing our things, calmly waiting
Now praying we can just return
To homes as planned.
Understand?

(Look)

Look in the eyes
to realize
hope still
lives inside

RIDE ALONG

Officer Mike was on the track team over at Douglass High

He ran pretty fast, finished 4th in his
class. A smart super nice guy.

No one was surprised he joined the force
close to his own neighborhood.

Homes, most in shambles, low-incomes; grandmas.
Teens 'up to no good'.

Call came "group of truants out on the
street not in their own public school".

Mike quickly spots them. They're just three. He got them.
Staring at Yield and Stop signs.

Something different. Deliberate. Not least bit belligerent.
More awkward than possibly high.

Mike was ready to run after as cops normally did.
But he recognized them said
"So, what's up kids ?"

They immediately reached in their pockets and
what they pulled out made him laugh

A ruler, protractor, compass for Geometry.
Homeschoolers were out doing Math.

NO IDEA

She is here and can hear you
Just no idea what you mean
You are too mean.
You are too shiny
Too far away. Not clearly seen.

Come closer, she will zap you
Or slap at you just the same.
Handicapped and harmless.
Ask her name.

ACCESS SUCCESS

One of us in every office
Just lower cabinets; each

Open wider entry doors
Put phones within my reach

Whatever you have to say
Sign or say it to my face

And no matter how
tempted you are

Don't take my parking space

QUALS

Uneducated regulated
Bare arms bearing arms

Shoot
Smart
Sharp militia

Always Right
Causing alarm

To hunt for sport
To cut life short

Recoil React Re-run

Militia; educate them
All
The 2nd right's begun

AGRONOMY

Sugar filled legumes

are tasty and sweet

Skills to plant fields

means a lifetime

to eat!

Further research

Agronomy so

Sweet seeds can

sprout as you

learn, taste and grow

RESUSCITATION

Sometimes,
I can't breathe
So I have to

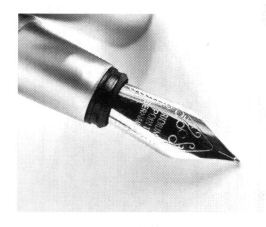

grab a Pen
To
Exhale

NO PRESSURE

Just the world.
Only
The universe

Insists the scribes
Imbibe

Dalliance
And dance around
And over
through.
Aside

The murk of hatred
Hurt and
Heartfelt horror

Dry eyed
Whetted
By feigned indifference

Searching for real.
Life.
With fake fingers
Trying to grasp
A pen and then

Enunciate.
And articulate .

*"A body
gesticulating..."*

Dictating the story
Dateline.
With a countdown
Of breaths

*"Under pressure
Under foot..."*

(now underground)

And so the scribe
Must describe

Chronicle crisis
And remove self
From the story

For the glory
Of the "bye" lines
By the deadline.

Then go hide.

POTHOLES

Where you choose to stand

does matter

Sitting down makes puddles splat

Jumping over turns into a game

We have had enough of that

Driving through simply disperses

Looking away has gotten old

Finally address the problems

Educate.

Fill in the holes.

PRUNING

Trimming saplings is easier
Than the felling of trees

Both start from
the planting of seeds

Proper water procedures
Most likely produce

The heartiest growths
Guarantee

Likewise with the children
All seedlings at birth

No potential differential
Pure gaiety and mirth
(tee hee hee)

FULL/FILLED

we're topped off
no more vacancies

all sold out
no standing room

not even making
waiting list

posting no sign

"returning soon"

the border's closed
the wall is built

it is up
it's very high

taking no more
applications

any pending
get denied

banning scammers,
hatred, ignorance,

racists, looters, fools

only allowing investors
in schools

ALL HIS

All that I know God taught me

All that I own God bought me

All that I have God gave me

All that I am God made me

Printed in the United States
by Baker & Taylor Publisher Services